INTO THE

INTO THE LONG GRASS

With Texts & Poems by

ALEX MARTIN

KIT WRIGHT

SIMON RAE

NEIL ROLLINSON

Images by

DAVID INSHAW

TOP EDGE PRESS

Jousting at Brydian

Every year, around Midsummer's Day, we set out: a team of irregulars, poets and boozers, touring Dorset. We live in pubs and meadows. We become wild men, on the run from time and the city.

On the third day we play cricket at Littlebredy. The ground is a tilted bowl scooped out of the chalk uplands. It is soft yet deeply carved, like the V in a woman's ribs, below the swell of her breasts. It has something of that magnetism too.

Beside the ground is a lake, where the feminine geology goes on underwater, fed by a hidden spring. All around, grassy slopes curve up towards the sky. Cattle graze in the shadows. Heat and light are trapped there, sweet with the scent of summer leaves and flowers.

We meet at the pavilion, a faded blue shack with white doors and windows. Its rooms smell of petrol, leather, cut grass and tobacco. Old team photographs and tea rotas are flyposted around the timber partitions, and an atmosphere of the 1940s pervades: the cars outside turn into Spitfires, and the captain's talk, filtered through the silence, is Churchill's voice crackling through the radio. Time has slowed to the speed of treacle oozing from a drum.

We change into cricketing gear: shirts and trousers every shade of white from chalk to rind of stilton, a jumble of other teams' caps. As we clatter across the floor in our spiked boots, we become players of a different sort, figures in an ancient mystery, knights walking stiffly out to the joust.

Outside, the stage is set. A crater of stubble, brilliantly lit. The first two batsmen crush their cigarettes underfoot and stride out, arms swinging.

The game begins. A ritual with familiar moves, yet infinite surprises and variations: cloud, sun, breeze, the unpredictable flight of a ball bouncing jaggedly off the turf or clobbered in a whistling arc through the hot sky. Every moment is unique and requires your attention.

There is a stillness here. An equilibrium. Balanced at the high point of summer, between light and shadow, time and no-time. A presence too, dimly audible in the silence of the valley: the scrape of the plough through chalky soil, sheep's teeth tearing the grass, echoes of forgotten wars. As if the air were laced with vapours of lotus-fruit, we become drunk on it, forgetful, happy as Circe's pigs among the clefts and swellings of the earth. Everything beyond the horizon is a dream.

*

On stuffy August afternoons back in Oxford, I read C. J. Bailey's *The Bride Valley* and Bill Putnam's *Roman Dorset*. I come across a phrase from W. G. Hoskins, 'the observables of England, and the secret history that lies behind them'.

I learn that the River Bride, which rises at Littlebredy, is just six and a half miles long, yet contains an entire river system in miniature. Its source is beneath the lake, which was dug out in 1800 as an ornament to Bridehead, the stately grey house that overlooks the cricket ground. The river runs down the valley, then dives underground again, before entering the sea through a bed of shingle near Bridport. So both its source and its mouth are hidden from the eye.

In the surrounding hills is a remarkable density of sacred sites: burial mounds, stone circles and ritual earthworks. They date from 3000 to 1000 BC, the earliest of them contemporary with the Pyramids of Giza. Two thirds of Dorset's prehistoric monuments are within four miles of this valley.

There are hill-forts built by the Durotriges, a Celtic tribe who left no writing, but whose coins and jewellery are ornamented with precise and finely worked designs. The name 'Durotriges' has survived only by chance, in two sources – writings by Roman soldiers found at Hadrian's Wall, and a history written in Alexandria in the first century AD.

The Romans destroyed the Durotriges and their culture, conquering the area in 43 AD. They built roads and camps, still visible in odd turf-covered quadrangles across the landscape. They collected taxes, traded, married, settled and farmed.

In 892, long after the Romans had gone, King Alfred built the Burghal Hidage, a line of fortresses to defend England from the Vikings. One of these was 'Brydian' – never identified, but the name echoes 'Bride' and 'Bredy', and it could be the hill-fort that looks down on Littlebredy from the south.

In 987, Earl Aethelmaer gave Littlebredy to Cerne Abbey. For 500 years, its sheep and oxen, its crops and barns and mills, belonged to the monks who lived under the sign of the club-wielding priapic giant at Cerne.

The Abbey was dissolved in 1544. Its lands were sold off. For two and a half centuries private owners came and went. Robert Williams, a local shipowner, bought Littlebredy in 1797. He built Bridehead house, landscaped the gardens, dammed the river to form the lake. Over the next century, his descendants turned the village into a model community. They built workers' cottages, a school, a new church. In the 1880s, they laid out a cricket pitch and added a new wing to Bridehead – big enough for two teams of players, together with scorers and umpires: a house party of 26 guests.

In the 1970s, David Inshaw came to this valley and painted 'The Cricket Game'. The picture captures many magical things: a brilliant blue sky streaked with white cirrus, sunlight and deep shadow on the Dorset hills, the drama on the cricket field, where men like figures on a living clock act out the harvest of the minutes and hours. Everywhere a mysterious radiance. 'The observables of England' are all there. So, by the painter's alchemy, is 'the secret history that lies behind them'.

His picture brought us here. He plays too, one of the irregulars, laying his brushes aside for more rustic weaponry.

Facts say little, but they say something. For five thousand years, people have come to this place. They set up, according to their understanding, stone circles, fortresses, houses and farms. We make a homage of our own: a bundle of poems and pictures, 'Dorset' inked into next year's diary, a game of cricket on Midsummer's Day.

ALEX MARTIN

Littlebredy

At the top of the hill the twisted thorns
Were crouching out of the way of the wind
That raced in over the miles of shivering furze.
The valley air
Was sweet with the honey of yellow-beaked flowers
And across the lake the house
Stared at itself in the olive water.

What had been remembered
By the folk intelligence of the path
That chose that way of all ways through the trees?
Why had the dreaming ice
In the slumbering glacier warmed toward this shape,
Beyond all others,
To hollow out its inclination?

Everything there knew why,
However,
The white-robed cricketers, inexorably,
Had made their way down into the valley
To do their dance of stillness;
To do their courtly dance of almost stillness,
Dancing upon their graves before they died.

KIT WRIGHT

Scoring A Six At Little Bredy:

Sonnet instruction manual

Bind up a creaky heart of cork in shroud-scraps
Of lost loves, ghost lives. Knot tight with twine;
Encase between two neatly taken scalps
Tanned to the colour of a vintage wine.

Shape with sharp hammer taps, then sew
The grinning death's-head stitches of the seam.
Lacquer thinly with bravado; throw
To the fastest bowler on the opposing team.

Then while he strides towards his distant mark
Take guard, and draw the courage to stand fast
From ancient but unbowed trees around the park.
For once, let life swing with the grain, and blast

The scab-red cannonball vertiginously high
Into a far corner of the evening sky.

SIMON RAE

Il Pomseroso

Far from all resort of mirth
Save the cricket

MILTON

Shaken out of the little tin box
Of the pavilion like dice
Onto the green baize, we roll
And gambol, happy as matelots
On shore leave. A sea shanty
Rises half formed to my lips.
We have been drinking.
The song could celebrate this fact.
I begin to hum experimentally,
Making ticks in the air
With my right forefinger.
But who is this, billowing
In his white coat down the steps
Like a ship under full sail?
With an easel of awkward kindling
Slipping under his arm, he could be
An artist about to set up shop.
Perhaps he would like to install
A naked model among us.
(We'd like this too.) Instead,
He steers us all out into the bay
Followed in turn by two
Helmeted Argonauts
Paddling their coracles of shadow.

Leave me here in the shallows,
A willing castaway.
From this safe distance
I can admire the tableau
Of flickering forms, like Shadrach,
Meshach and Abednego
Playing tip-and-run in the fiery furnace.
Or, still humming an early draft
Of my catch, lose myself
In the steepling fathoms
Of the clear blue sky.
From which, without warning,
Beyond a broadside of fiendish
Howls, catastrophe, in the shape
Of a stray carrion cannonball,
Swoops screaming straight
Out of the sun's unforgiving eye
Ripping through the hastily hoisted
Rigging of fingers.
The impact startles the afternoon
From its torpor. Kites slide
Off their invisible shelves.
Woodpigeons explode
Through the heavy branches
In feathery alarm. Holed
Amidships, I am sunk
And sink to my knees.
The captain is beside himself.

I close an eye to bring him into line,
Then, with an expiatory wave,
Begin to wade through the outfield's
Seven seas. The scorers sit
At their table chatting and sipping,
An image of a sanctuary.
There I am bound. A lifetime later,
Skin calloused, hair bleached white
And beard between my knees,
I stumble up the punitive incline,
And, with a last gasp,
Clasp the neck of the bottle
I was always confident would contain
A message just for me.

SIMON RAE

Cricket Haiku

(A Seasonal Cycle)

Snow and pear blossom
falling at tea – we huddle
over the cream scones.

Between two overs
the song of the first cuckoo
passes unnoticed.

Rain stops play, again –
I watch the seagulls wading
at deep mid wicket.

A sudden cloudburst –
twenty two men sheltering
under the elm trees.

Exploding acorns
under the groundsman's roller –
snap crackle and pop.

A ring of pale grass –
the ghost of the boundary rope
fading day by day.

Under the hedge
ten cricket balls over winter –
a score of sixty.

A snowman melting
at deep mid wicket, its eyes
two stones in the grass.

Midwinter silence,
the pavilion sits tight
against the snow fall.

NEIL ROLLINSON

Still-life With Cricketers

Almost timeless you'd think,
the way the fields and valleys
lie like this, an emerald hollow
set in the Dorset hills,
a game of cricket under the high sun,
theatre of idle dreams, tomfoolery:
batters and bowlers, dozy fielders
nursing their hangovers,
every shade and half shade of green
shifting in sunlight and shadow,
the shimmer of moth wing, wasp
and grasshopper, the constant buzz
of insect life; wives and girlfriends
sprawl on the grass, snoozing,
or watching the match, the call
of a buzzard circling overhead,
dead centre of everything,
its kingdom of hedgerow, brambles
and oak, this snapshot of England,
so calm a single dog bark
echoes off three different hills,
you lift your head and catch it like this:
green on green, the white of a lake,
the red blur of a cricket ball high in the sky,
and a daytime moon, suspended like ice
in a beaker of blue gin.

NEIL ROLLINSON

The Roller In The Woods

Who would imagine a cricket ground
Had ever existed here,
Folded into a farm on the downland pasture,
Lapping the edge of the oakwood
And the buttercup-quilted rides?

For the Toll is returned to plough
After a century of combat,
Sown to a sea of blue-green waves
Beneath which it lies drowned.
And now,
Stick nor stone of the old pavilion,
Hook nor slat of the scoreboard left:
Never an echo of tumbling children,
Tattle of Edwardians,
Knocking their pipes out on the rough deal benches.

Foaming hawthorn and rhododendron
Have colonised the field-edge, spreading
Through copper beech and flowering chestnut
And adventitious saplings.

Where

Is the *camaraderie*
Of the side I played for so often here:

Their thunderous blows and heroical overs,
The days that flowed with sun and wind:
Stalemates in dismal drizzle,
And the finger of death uplifted in the dusk?

Where,
I might ask,
Are Nobby and Dave and the Colonel and Phil,
The two Pauls and the one and only
Moggy Worsfold and Arthur Spark?
I have failed to raise them,
By staring out at the level meadow
As if I were Cadmus who had sown
The dragon's teeth and awaited
His armed men springing from the earth.

But I did untangle my way
Through the canopied darkness of what had been
The boundary. Among the laurel bushes
And snagging goose-grass and rabbit holes,
I found what I'd forgotten, hidden
Under a wide oak. For this

Was what they could not lightly move
In the rhythm of abandonment:
Here was the deep ground-bass and the solemn
Measure of constancy, foundry-born,
That had lasted so long.

And I laid
My arms across the surface, feeling
Under the rust and dust and pollen,
The summers that never seemed to move
And all the years gone by to the creak of iron.

KIT WRIGHT

David Inshaw: *The Cricket Game III*

2014

Published in 2022 by Top Edge Press
Loudon, Little Tew, Chipping Norton, Oxfordshire OX7 4JJ

'Littlebredy' & 'The Roller in the Woods' first appeared in Kit Wright's collection,
Ode To Didcot Power Station (Bloodaxe Books 2014)

ISBN: 978-0-9545495-7-2

Designed by Libanus Press Ltd, Marlborough
Printed in the UK